REWIRED FOR SECURE ATTACHMENT

BREAK FREE FROM ANXIETY AND AVOIDANCE, HEAL CHILDHOOD WOUNDS, AND ATTRACT THE LOVE YOU DESERVE IN 30 DAYS

ELLIOT CHASE

CONTENTS

INTRODUCTION

THE PATTERN THAT CHANGED EVERYTHING

Linda sat in her car outside her ex-boyfriend's apartment, staring at the darkened windows and feeling a familiar ache in her chest. Three relationships, three years, three devastating endings—all eerily similar. Each man had started out charming and attentive, drawing her in with intense connection and promises of forever. But as soon as she began to feel secure, to believe this might be "the one," they would begin to pull away.

The texts became shorter. The dates less frequent. The emotional walls went up, brick by brick, until she was left grasping at someone who had become a stranger.

What haunted her most wasn't just the heartbreak—it was the recognition. The same desperate anxiety that made her check her phone obsessively. The same overwhelming need for reassurance that seemed to push partners away. The same crushing fear of abandonment that became a self-fulfilling prophecy.

She wasn't just unlucky in love. She was trapped in a pattern so precise it felt scripted.

That night, Linda made a discovery that would change her life forever. Through tears and Google searches at 2 AM, she stumbled upon research about attachment theory and the neuroscience of love. What she learned shook her to her core: her childhood experiences—growing up with a mother who was loving one moment and emotionally distant the next—had literally rewired her brain for insecurity.

But here's what gave her hope: if her brain had been wired for insecurity, it could be rewired for security. Her love life wasn't doomed by her past—it was simply operating from an outdated blueprint that could be rewritten.

YOUR 30-DAY TRANSFORMATION AWAITS

This book exists for one transformative purpose: to provide you with a scientifically-backed, step-by-step process that rewires your attachment system from insecurity to security in just 30 days. Not through years of therapy, not through hoping the "right person" will fix you, but through targeted daily practices that literally change how your brain processes love, connection, and relationships.

For too long, people struggling with relationship patterns have been told to "just choose better partners" or "work on your self-esteem." While well-intentioned, this advice misses the deeper truth: your relationship struggles aren't character flaws or conscious choices—they're the result of neural pathways carved by early experiences.

This book bridges the gap between understanding why you struggle and actually changing those patterns. You'll discover:

- How to identify the specific ways your nervous system has been programmed for insecurity

- The exact techniques needed to create new neural pathways for secure attachment
- Daily practices that will make these changes permanent

The goal isn't just to stop destructive patterns—it's to help you break free from anxious and avoidant relationship cycles, heal deep childhood wounds, and develop the inner security needed to attract confident, healthy love.

WHO THIS BOOK SERVES

This book is specifically designed for adults who recognize themselves in Linda's story—those trapped in cycles of relationship anxiety, emotional avoidance, or consistently attracting partners who can't meet their needs for genuine connection.

You might become anxiously attached in relationships, constantly seeking reassurance or feeling consumed by fears of abandonment. Perhaps you recognize avoidant patterns—pulling away when relationships get close or feeling suffocated by emotional needs. Or maybe you're caught in the painful dance of anxious-avoidant relationships, repeatedly drawn to emotionally unavailable partners.

This book is for you if you're tired of surface-level advice that doesn't address root causes. You've probably tried positive thinking, dating apps, or therapy, but you keep finding yourself in the same patterns with different people.

You're ready to go deeper than behavioral changes.

Most importantly, this is for those ready to do the inner work required for lasting change. You don't need to be perfect—you just need to be ready to heal the childhood wounds that have been unconsciously directing your adult relationships.

THE NEUROSCIENCE ADVANTAGE

Unlike traditional relationship advice that focuses on communication techniques, this book addresses the neurobiological foundation of how you experience love and connection. Most relationship guidance treats symptoms without addressing the underlying cause: an insecurely wired nervous system.

Here's what makes this approach revolutionary: we're literally rewiring the neural pathways in your brain that determine how you attach to others. Using cutting-edge research in neuroscience, attachment theory, and trauma healing, you'll work directly with your nervous system to create lasting change from the inside out.

When you change behaviors without addressing underlying neural patterns, old programming eventually resurfaces, especially under stress. But when you rewire your attachment system at the neurological level, the changes become your new default operating system.

This isn't about managing insecurities—it's about eliminating them at their source.

YOUR JOURNEY AHEAD

Over the next 30 days, you'll be guided through four distinct transformation phases:

Days 1-7: Recognition and Regulation - Identify your specific attachment patterns and learn nervous system regulation techniques.

Days 8-14: Rewiring and Release - Interrupt old neural pathways while creating new ones through targeted healing exercises.

Days 15-21: Integration and Embodiment - Make secure attachment your default mode through daily practices.

Days 22-30: Mastery and Maintenance - Solidify transformation and prepare for long-term success.

Each day includes specific exercises, journal prompts, and mini-lessons taking 15-30 minutes to complete. You'll read real stories of successful transformation, understand simple neuroscience explanations, and track measurable progress.

YOUR MOMENT OF CHOICE

Right now, you're standing at a crossroads. Behind you lies a trail of relationship patterns that have brought pain and disappointment. Ahead lies the possibility of complete transformation—not just better relationships, but a fundamentally different way of experiencing love.

The next 30 days will pass whether you choose transformation or remain stuck in familiar patterns.

How many more relationships will you watch crumble under unhealed attachment wounds? How much longer will you accept anxiety and avoidance as normal parts of love?

The transformation waiting isn't just about finding a better partner—it's about becoming the securely attached person who naturally attracts and maintains healthy love. Your future self, the one who loves confidently and creates relationships built on genuine security rather than fear, is waiting just 30 days from now.

Turn the page, and let's begin.

1
THE GHOST IN YOUR LOVE STORY

THE HIDDEN MAP YOUR CHILDHOOD DREW

Imagine a three-year-old Jennifer crying in her crib, calling for her overwhelmed mother who is dealing with her own depression and rarely responds with warmth or consistency. This little girl's developing brain is making crucial decisions about love, safety, and whether she can count on others to be there for her. These early experiences create an invisible blueprint that will guide every romantic relationship she enters for decades to come.

Your attachment blueprint is the unconscious template your brain developed in your earliest years to navigate relationships and ensure survival. Formed through thousands of micro-interactions with your primary caregivers before age five, this blueprint operates like invisible software running in the background of every romantic encounter.

The science behind this process is both fascinating and sobering:

- Critical period formation: The attachment system develops during the most neuroplastic period of human development, when your brain is forming 700-1000 new neural connections per second
- Survival-based programming: Your young brain prioritized survival over accuracy, creating strategies that kept you safe as a child but may sabotage adult relationships
- Implicit memory storage: These patterns are stored in implicit memory, meaning they influence your behavior without conscious awareness

Consider Mason, who came to therapy convinced he was "just bad at relationships." At 34, his pattern was always the same: intense initial connection, followed by a growing sense of suffocation, then an inevitable breakup where he'd cite "needing space." Through exploring his childhood, he discovered that his emotionally intrusive mother had trained his nervous system to associate closeness with losing himself.

His attachment blueprint had learned that love meant engulfment.

So his brain would trigger escape responses whenever relationships deepened. Once he understood this wasn't a character flaw but a protective mechanism formed decades earlier, he could begin the work of rewiring these automatic responses.

Your blueprint isn't your fault, but it is your responsibility to understand and transform it. In the next chapter, we'll explore exactly how these early experiences shaped your specific attachment style and why your heart learned to protect itself in the particular ways it did.

YOUR BRAIN'S FIRST SURVIVAL LESSONS

Picture a baby's brain as a construction site where the foreman (your caregiver's responses) determines which neural pathways get built into superhighways and which remain dirt roads. When Elliott was an infant and his anxious father would tense up every time he cried, his developing nervous system learned to read tension as danger, creating hypervigilant neural pathways that would later manifest as relationship anxiety.

Your early bonding experiences literally shaped your brain architecture, determining which neural networks became dominant and how your nervous system learned to respond to connection, separation, and emotional intimacy. Understanding this neuroscience is crucial because it explains why changing relationship patterns requires more than willpower—it requires rewiring deeply embedded neural pathways.

The key mechanisms behind this process include:

- Mirror neuron development: Your brain's mirror neurons learned to read and respond to your caregiver's emotional states, creating your baseline for what feels "normal" in relationships
- Stress response calibration: Your autonomic nervous system calibrated its threat detection based on early experiences, determining your window of tolerance for relationship stress
- Neuroplasticity and hope: While these patterns run deep, adult neuroplasticity means your brain can form new neural pathways with conscious effort and repeated positive experiences

Consider Violet, who struggled with what she called "relationship paranoia"—constantly scanning her partner's face for signs of rejection, interpreting neutral expressions as anger, and feeling flooded with anxiety when her boyfriend seemed distant. Brain scans of people with her attachment style show hyperactivity in the amygdala (fear center) and heightened sensitivity in areas that process social threats.

Her brain had been trained by an unpredictably angry father to treat ambiguous social cues as potential danger.

Understanding that her "paranoia" was actually her brain doing exactly what it had been trained to do helped her develop compassion for her responses while working to retrain her neural pathways through secure relationship experiences.

This isn't about blame or dwelling in the past. It's about understanding the invisible operating system that's been running your relationships so you can consciously upgrade it. In the next chapter, we'll explore the specific ways your heart learned to protect itself and how these protective strategies became the very barriers keeping love at arm's length.

YOUR ATTACHMENT BLUEPRINT REVEALS EVERYTHING

Sarah sat across from her fifth therapist in ten years, describing yet another relationship that had followed the exact same script: passionate beginning, gradual emotional withdrawal from her partner, her increasing pursuit and anxiety, followed by an explosive fight that ended everything. "It's like I'm cursed," she said, not realizing she was describing the precise signature of anxious attachment playing out with clockwork predictability.

Your attachment style creates a recognizable signature—a consistent pattern of thoughts, feelings, and behaviors that shows up across all your romantic relationships. Learning to recognize your signature is like becoming aware of your own accent; once you hear it, you can't unhear it, and this awareness becomes the first step toward change.

The key elements that reveal your attachment blueprint include:

- Predictable emotional patterns: Each attachment style has characteristic emotional responses to relationship milestones, conflicts, and intimacy that repeat with remarkable consistency
- Unconscious partner selection: Your attachment system draws you toward partners who will recreate familiar dynamics, even when those dynamics are painful
- Self-fulfilling prophecies: Your attachment-driven behaviors often create the very outcomes you fear most, reinforcing your core beliefs about relationships

Consider Marcus, who realized his attachment signature when he noticed he only felt passionate attraction to women who were emotionally unavailable. His avoidant attachment style had trained him to equate safety with distance, so available, loving women felt "boring" while unavailable ones felt exciting.

He would pursue these unavailable women intensely, but the moment they became interested and available, his attraction would die.

His signature included: immediate chemistry with distant partners, loss of interest when pursuit ended, and a deep fear of being "trapped" in committed relationships. Recognizing this pattern allowed him to make conscious choices rather than being driven by unconscious programming.

Your attachment blueprint isn't destiny—it's simply the starting point for your transformation. By understanding how your early experiences shaped your relationship patterns, you gain the power to rewrite them. In Chapter Two, we'll dive deeper into the specific ways your heart learned to protect itself and why these protective strategies became the very walls keeping true intimacy out.

WHEN TRUST FEELS LIKE A LUXURY

Daniel calculated that he'd spent over $50,000 on dates, relationship coaching, and therapy over five years, desperately trying to find lasting love while his insecure attachment system sabotaged every promising connection. But the financial cost paled in comparison to the emotional toll: the crushing loneliness, the constant anxiety about whether he was loveable, and the growing fear that he might spend his life alone.

Living with an insecure attachment system exacts a profound cost across multiple domains of your life. Beyond the obvious relationship struggles, insecure attachment affects your mental health, physical wellbeing, career success, and overall life satisfaction. Understanding these costs can provide motivation for the challenging but rewarding work of healing your attachment wounds.

The hidden price of unhealed attachment wounds includes:

- Emotional and mental health impact: Insecure attachment correlates with higher rates of anxiety, depression, and emotional dysregulation, as your nervous system remains chronically activated
- Physical health consequences: Chronic relationship stress and nervous system dysregulation contribute to inflammation, compromised immune function, and stress-related health issues
- Life limitation and missed opportunities: Insecure attachment patterns often lead to avoiding vulnerability, limiting career advancement, friendship depth, and life experiences that require emotional risk

Consider Rachel, who came to understand that her anxious attachment wasn't just affecting her love life—it was costing her everything. Her constant worry about relationships made it hard to focus at work, limiting her career advancement. She'd turned down job opportunities that required travel because she couldn't bear to be away from partners who might leave.

Her friendships suffered because she was always crisis-managing romantic relationships.

Most painfully, she'd terminated a pregnancy two years earlier because her relationship felt too unstable to bring a child into, a decision that haunted her daily. The cost of unhealed attachment wounds extended far beyond dating—it was shaping every major life decision and limiting her ability to create the life she truly wanted.

But here's what's possible: secure attachment isn't just about finding love—it's about reclaiming your entire life. When you heal these deep patterns, you don't just get better relationships; you get better everything. In Chapter Two, we'll explore how your protective strategies formed and why understanding them is the key to freedom.

WHEN YOUR BRAIN BREAKS DATING RULES

Marcus had read every dating book, followed every "rule," and could recite dating advice like scripture: "Don't text back too quickly," "Play hard to get," "Wait three dates before sleeping together." But none of it worked because traditional dating advice assumes you have secure attachment wiring. When your nervous system is programmed for insecurity, following surface-level strategies is like trying to run new software on a computer with a corrupted operating system.

Traditional dating advice fails for people with insecure attachment because it addresses symptoms rather than root causes. These approaches assume that relationship problems stem from not knowing the "right" techniques, when in reality, they stem from unconscious attachment programming that overrides conscious strategies. Until you address the underlying wiring, you'll continue to sabotage your own efforts despite knowing all the "rules."

Why conventional wisdom falls short:

- Surface solutions for deep problems: Most dating advice focuses on behavior modification without addressing the underlying nervous system patterns driving those behaviors
- One-size-fits-all approaches ignore attachment differences: Advice that works for secure individuals often backfires for those with anxious or avoidant attachment styles
- Cognitive strategies vs. nervous system realities: Your attachment system operates faster than conscious thought, meaning willpower and "positive thinking" are no match for deeply ingrained survival programming

Consider Jessica, who followed her dating coach's advice to "be mysterious" and wait hours before responding to texts, but her anxious attachment made this torture. She'd spend those hours obsessing, checking her phone constantly, and spiraling into anxiety about whether she was playing the game right.

When she finally sent carefully crafted "cool" responses, they felt so inauthentic that they created distance rather than attraction.

The advice wasn't wrong—it just wasn't designed for someone whose nervous system interpreted delayed responses as potential abandonment. She needed attachment-informed strategies that worked with her wiring rather than against it, helping her develop genuine security rather than performing unavailability while feeling desperate inside.

Your attachment blueprint doesn't make you broken—it makes you human. But understanding how it operates gives you the power to work with your nervous system instead of against it, creating authentic connection rather than performing strategies that feel foreign to your core.

2
WHEN YOUR HEART LEARNED TO HIDE

TRACING YOUR EMOTIONAL WOUNDS THROUGH TIME

Imagine a young child's heart as a tender seedling, naturally reaching toward the sun of love and connection. But what happens when that sun becomes unpredictable—sometimes warm, sometimes scorching, sometimes absent entirely? The seedling learns to adapt, to protect itself, to survive. This is how your attachment injuries began, not as dramatic single events, but as patterns woven into the fabric of your earliest relationships.

Your attachment injury timeline isn't just a collection of memories; it's the blueprint your nervous system created for navigating love and safety. Understanding this timeline allows you to see how your current relationship patterns aren't character flaws or personal failures, but intelligent adaptations that once served to protect you.

The wounds that shape your adult relationships typically develop across three critical periods:

- Early infancy patterns (0-2 years): How your caregivers responded to your basic needs for comfort, feeding, and soothing created your first templates for trust and safety
- Toddlerhood dynamics (2-4 years): The way your emerging autonomy was met—with encouragement or control, patience or frustration—shaped your beliefs about independence within relationships
- School-age experiences (5-12 years): Family dynamics, parental stress, divorce, or emotional unavailability during these formative years created deeper attachment wounds that now influence your adult relationship choices

Emily came to therapy convinced she was "just bad at relationships." As we mapped her attachment timeline, she discovered that her pattern of intense initial connection followed by sudden withdrawal wasn't a personality flaw. At age seven, her mother had suffered severe depression after her father left. Emily learned that getting too close to someone meant risking devastating abandonment.

Her adult pattern of sabotaging relationships just as they deepened was her nervous system's way of controlling the timing of inevitable loss—leaving before being left.

Understanding this timeline helped her recognize something crucial. Her relationship struggles weren't evidence of her inadequacy, but proof of her childhood resilience.

When you trace your own emotional wounds through time, you begin to see the logic behind patterns that once seemed random or self-destructive. This understanding becomes the foundation for the rewiring work we'll explore in Chapter 3, where we'll examine how these early adaptations create the anxiety-avoidance dance that keeps secure love at arm's length.

WHEN YOUR BODY LEARNED TO FEAR

There's often a pivotal moment—or series of moments—when a child's nervous system makes a fundamental shift from expecting safety to scanning for danger. This isn't always dramatic abuse or neglect; sometimes it's as subtle as a parent's chronic anxiety, a family's financial stress, or the emotional unavailability that comes with depression or addiction. In that moment, your nervous system learned that love and safety were scarce resources that couldn't be counted on.

This neurobiological shift from safety to scarcity becomes the lens through which you view all future relationships. Your nervous system, having learned that connection equals potential threat, begins to treat love as something dangerous rather than nourishing. This creates the fundamental contradiction that plagues adult relationships: desperately wanting connection while simultaneously bracing for its loss.

The ghost patterns we explored in Chapter 1 are actually your nervous system's protective responses, encoded in your body during these early moments of threat. These patterns manifest in three primary ways:

- Hypervigilance in relationships: Constantly scanning for signs of rejection, criticism, or abandonment, even in secure partnerships
- Scarcity mindset about love: Believing that affection, attention, and care are limited resources that must be earned or could be withdrawn at any moment
- Safety through control: Attempting to manage relationship outcomes through people-pleasing, emotional withdrawal, or creating conflict to maintain familiar distance

Alexander described his childhood home as "walking on eggshells." His father wasn't abusive, but his unpredictable moods meant that the same behavior might be met with laughter one day and explosive anger the next. By age ten, Alexander had become hyperattuned to micro-expressions and voice tones, constantly adjusting his behavior to maintain peace.

In his adult relationships, this translated into exhausting hypervigilance—analyzing every text message for hidden meaning, interpreting normal relationship conflicts as signs of impending breakup, and shape-shifting to be whoever he thought his partner wanted. His nervous system had learned that safety required constant performance, making authentic intimacy feel impossibly dangerous.

Understanding when and how your body learned to fear connection is crucial for the rewiring process ahead. In Chapter 3, we'll explore how this fear manifests as the anxiety-avoidance tango that keeps you trapped in unfulfilling relationship patterns, dancing between desperate pursuit and protective withdrawal.

WHEN PROTECTION BECOMES SELF-DESTRUCTION

The strategies that helped you survive childhood often become the very patterns that sabotage your adult relationships. What once protected a vulnerable child now creates the disconnection and conflict you're desperately trying to avoid. These aren't conscious choices but deeply embedded neural pathways that activate automatically when your nervous system perceives relationship threat.

Understanding how your survival strategies operate in adult relationships is crucial for breaking free from repetitive patterns. These strategies were brilliant adaptations that kept you safe when you were small and powerless, but they now create the very outcomes you fear most: rejection, abandonment, and emotional distance.

The ghost patterns from Chapter 1 typically manifest through three primary survival strategies:

- The people-pleaser: Learned that compliance and perfection could sometimes earn love and avoid conflict, but now struggles with resentment and loss of authentic self in relationships
- The withdrawer: Discovered that emotional distance provided protection from unpredictable caregivers, but now creates the abandonment they fear by pushing partners away
- The controller: Found that managing others' emotions or behaviors created temporary safety, but now suffocates relationships with micromanagement and anxiety

Daisy was known among her friends as the "perfect girlfriend"—always accommodating, never demanding, endlessly supportive. But her relationships followed a predictable pattern: initial adoration from partners who loved her easy-going nature, followed by their gradual loss of respect and interest, and finally their departure for someone who seemed more challenging and authentic.

Her childhood survival strategy of earning love through perfection had become a relationship trap. She attracted people who wanted a caretaker rather than a partner, then felt invisible and resentful when they took her selflessness for granted. Her fear of conflict, which had protected her from her father's rage, now prevented her from having the healthy boundaries necessary for lasting love.

Recognition is the first step toward transformation. When you can see your protective patterns clearly, without judgment, you create space for new choices. These survival strategies aren't character flaws—they're evidence of your resilience and adaptability.

In Chapter 3, we'll explore how these protective patterns create the anxiety-avoidance dance that keeps you cycling between desperate pursuit and defensive withdrawal, never finding the secure connection your heart truly craves.

UNCOVERING YOUR HIDDEN EMOTIONAL ARMOR

Beneath all the various relationship struggles and patterns lies your core attachment wound—the fundamental fear or belief about yourself in relationship to others that was formed in your earliest experiences of love and care. This wound becomes the organizing principle around which all your protective mechanisms develop, like a psychological immune system designed to prevent re-injury.

Your core attachment wound isn't just an intellectual concept; it's a felt sense in your body, a contraction in your heart, a story your nervous system tells about what it means to be you in relationship with others. Identifying this wound allows you to understand why certain relationship triggers feel so disproportionately threatening and why your protective responses can be so intense.

The ghost patterns we explored in Chapter 1 typically organize around three primary core wounds:

- Core wounds of abandonment: "I am too much/not enough and will inevitably be left," leading to protective mechanisms of clinging, people-pleasing, or preemptive withdrawal
- Core wounds of engulfment: "Love means losing myself and being controlled," creating protective patterns of emotional distance, independence, or relationship sabotage
- Core wounds of betrayal: "People who say they love me will ultimately hurt me," resulting in protective hypervigilance, testing behaviors, or inability to fully trust

Marcus couldn't understand why he felt panicked whenever his partner wanted to spend more time together. Objectively, he loved her and wanted the relationship to deepen, but his body would flood with anxiety whenever she suggested moving in together or talked about future plans.

Through exploring his attachment history, he discovered his core wound of engulfment. His mother had been loving but suffocating, using him as her emotional confidant after his parents' divorce and becoming distressed whenever he showed independence. His protective mechanism was to maintain emotional and physical distance in relationships, sabotaging them whenever they moved toward the deeper commitment he consciously wanted.

Recognizing this pattern allowed him to distinguish between his wound-based fear and his authentic desires, creating space to respond rather than react.

Understanding your core attachment wound is like finding the master key to your relationship patterns. It explains why certain situations feel so threatening and why your nervous system mobilizes such intense protective responses. In Chapter 3, we'll explore how these wounds create the anxiety-avoidance dance that keeps secure love just out of reach.

3
THE ANXIETY-AVOIDANCE TANGO YOU CAN'T STOP DANCING

THE DANCE THAT TRAPS US

Remember those childhood wounds we explored in the last chapter? They don't just stay buried in your past. They come alive in your adult relationships, creating a destructive dance that feels impossible to stop.

The anxiety-avoidance dynamic creates a perfect storm of mutual triggering, where each partner's coping mechanism directly activates the other's deepest fears. This isn't coincidence—it's a psychological magnetism that draws anxious and avoidant types together like opposite poles of a magnet, creating an addictive cycle that feels like intense chemistry but is actually trauma bonding.

HOW THIS DANCE WORKS

Anxious attachment triggers avoidant withdrawal: The more an anxiously attached person seeks reassurance, closeness, and connection, the more overwhelmed and suffocated the avoidant partner feels, causing them to pull away or shut down emotionally.

Avoidant withdrawal triggers anxious pursuit: When the avoidant partner retreats, creates distance, or becomes emotionally unavailable, it confirms the anxious partner's deepest fear of abandonment, intensifying their pursuit and need for reassurance.

The dance escalates in intensity: Each person's coping mechanism becomes more extreme over time—the anxious partner becomes more clingy and demanding, while the avoidant partner becomes more distant and emotionally unavailable, creating a widening gap that neither knows how to bridge.

Mia met Cole at a coffee shop, and she was immediately drawn to his mysterious, independent energy. He seemed so self-assured, so different from her usual neediness in relationships. Cole, meanwhile, was attracted to her warmth and emotional expressiveness—something he felt he lacked.

Within months, their initial attraction had morphed into a painful cycle.

The more Mia tried to get close, asking about his day, wanting to spend time together, the more Cole felt overwhelmed and would work late or make plans with friends. Her attempts at connection felt like invasions to him, while his need for space felt like rejection to her.

Neither understood they were perfectly designed to trigger each other's attachment wounds.

This dance feels familiar because it mirrors the original relationships where you learned these patterns. Your nervous system recognizes the familiar chaos and mistakes it for love.

Tomorrow, we'll begin the rewiring process by meeting your nervous system face-to-face.

HOOKED ON TOXIC LOVE PATTERNS

Here's the thing about those painful relationship patterns you can't seem to break—your body is literally addicted to them.

Your nervous system becomes biochemically addicted to the stress hormones and neurochemicals produced by unstable relationships, creating a literal addiction to relationship drama that your brain interprets as "love" or "chemistry." This addiction makes calm, secure relationships feel boring or wrong, even when they're exactly what you consciously want.

THE BIOCHEMISTRY OF TOXIC LOVE

Trauma bonding through stress chemicals: The cycle of conflict and reconciliation floods your system with cortisol, adrenaline, and dopamine, creating an addictive high-low pattern that your brain learns to crave and associate with romantic love.

Think of it like a drug. The fight creates stress hormones that make everything feel intense and urgent. The makeup afterward floods you with relief chemicals that feel like pure bliss.

Intermittent reinforcement creates the strongest addiction: Just like gambling, the unpredictable nature of when you'll receive love, attention, or validation from an inconsistent partner creates the most powerful psychological addiction, making you chase the "high" of their approval even harder.

Secure love feels "flat" by comparison: When you're used to the biochemical rollercoaster of anxious-avoidant dynamics, healthy relationships can feel boring, lacking in passion, or "too easy," causing you to sabotage or leave relationships that would actually fulfill you.

Logan had been in therapy for two years, working on his avoidant patterns, when he met Sophia, a secure, emotionally available woman who was genuinely interested in him. She was consistent, kind, and didn't play games—everything he thought he wanted.

But after three months of dating, he found himself feeling restless and disconnected.

"She's amazing on paper," he told his therapist, "but I don't feel that spark, that intensity I'm used to." His nervous system, accustomed to the adrenaline rush of chasing unavailable women or being pursued by anxious partners, couldn't recognize the calm safety of secure love as desirable. The absence of drama registered as an absence of chemistry.

This is why you keep choosing the same type of person over and over again. Your wounded nervous system is running the show, not your conscious mind.

The good news? You can rewire this addiction. Starting next week, we'll teach your nervous system to recognize safety as attractive.

WHEN FEAR BECOMES YOUR DATING COMPASS

Here's what's really happening when you keep choosing the wrong people: your unconscious mind is using fear as a compass, leading you straight back to your original wounds.

Your unconscious mind is drawn to partners who will recreate your original attachment wounds, not to torture you, but in a misguided attempt to finally "win" the love that was withheld in childhood. This unconscious pattern keeps you choosing partners who are emotionally unavailable, inconsistent, or triggering in familiar ways.

WHY WE CHOOSE WHAT HURTS US

Childhood wounds seek familiar territory: Your psyche gravitates toward what feels "normal" based on your earliest relationships, even when that normal was painful, because the unknown feels more threatening than familiar pain.

It's like your nervous system has a broken GPS that thinks danger is home.

The unconscious belief that love must be earned: If you learned early that love was conditional, scarce, or required you to be "perfect," you'll unconsciously choose partners who make you work for their affection, believing this struggle proves the love is "real" or valuable.

Repetition compulsion seeks resolution: Your unconscious mind keeps choosing similar partners in an attempt to heal the original wound—if you can finally get this unavailable person to love you, it will prove you were worthy of love all along.

Diana grew up with a father who was emotionally distant and critical, always focused on work and rarely available for connection. Despite years of therapy and conscious awareness of this pattern, she found herself repeatedly attracted to men who were workaholics, emotionally unavailable, or withholding with affection.

Each time she met a man who was emotionally present and available, she felt uncomfortable and found reasons why he wasn't "right" for her. Her unconscious mind was still trying to win her father's love by choosing men who would require her to prove her worthiness, recreating the familiar dynamic where love felt scarce and had to be earned through perfect behavior.

This is why willpower and conscious choice aren't enough to break these patterns. Your nervous system is running a program installed decades ago, designed to keep you safe in a world that no longer exists.

The solution isn't to fight these patterns with logic. It's to rewire your nervous system at the root level, teaching it to recognize safety and security as attractive instead of threatening.

THE MAGNETIC DANCE OF ATTRACTION

What many people mistake for passionate chemistry is actually the neurological activation that occurs when your attachment system is triggered by inconsistency and uncertainty. True chemistry can exist without the push-pull dynamic, but it requires rewiring your nervous system to recognize safety and consistency as attractive rather than threatening.

DECODING FALSE CHEMISTRY

Intermittent reinforcement masquerades as passion: The unpredictable nature of when your partner will be available, loving, or attentive creates a dopamine hit that feels like intense attraction, but is actually your brain's response to uncertainty and the hope of reward.

Anxiety and arousal feel similar in the body: The physical sensations of anxiety—increased heart rate, butterflies, heightened alertness—can be easily confused with sexual and romantic attraction, leading you to believe that feeling nervous around someone means you're attracted to them.

Healthy chemistry feels different: Genuine chemistry combined with secure attachment creates a sense of energized calm, excitement without anxiety, and attraction that doesn't require drama or uncertainty to maintain its intensity.

Marcus described his relationship with Elena as "the most intense chemistry" he'd ever experienced. She was unpredictable—sometimes warm and affectionate, other times cold and distant. He never knew which version of her he'd encounter, and he found himself constantly thinking about her, analyzing her moods, trying to figure out how to keep her interested.

The uncertainty made every positive interaction feel like a victory, every smile feel like a gift.

When he finally started dating Rachel, who was consistently warm and available, he initially thought there was "no chemistry." It took months for him to realize that the absence of anxiety didn't mean the absence of attraction—it meant the presence of safety. Real chemistry, he learned, didn't require him to feel like he was constantly on the edge of losing someone.

You've now seen how your childhood wounds created an unconscious blueprint that keeps you trapped in the anxiety-avoidance dance. Your nervous system learned to mistake chaos for chemistry and struggle for love.

But here's the hope: every pattern you've learned can be unlearned.

Starting tomorrow, we begin the rewiring process. We'll teach your nervous system to recognize what safety actually feels like, so you can finally break free from these exhausting cycles and attract the secure love you truly deserve.

4
REWIRING DAY 1-7: MEETING YOUR NERVOUS SYSTEM

WHEN YOUR BODY REWRITES LOVE'S RULES

Your window of tolerance is like a thermostat for your emotional and physiological responses—it determines how much stress, excitement, or activation you can handle before your nervous system kicks into survival mode. When you're within this window, you can think clearly, respond rather than react, and maintain connection with others. Step outside it, and you're either in hyperarousal or hypoarousal.

This concept becomes crucial as you begin rewiring your attachment patterns because your nervous system holds the blueprint for how you experience love and connection.

UNDERSTANDING HYPERAROUSAL AND HYPOAROUSAL

Hyperarousal signals include racing heart, shallow breathing, feeling "wired," anxiety, anger, or the urge to escape or control situations.

Your body floods with stress hormones, preparing for fight or flight. In relationships, this might look like picking fights, becoming clingy, or feeling desperate for reassurance.

Hypoarousal patterns involve feeling numb, disconnected, foggy, exhausted, or like you're watching your life from outside your body. Your nervous system has essentially hit the brakes, shutting down to protect you. This shows up as emotional withdrawal, losing interest in your partner, or feeling nothing when they try to connect.

MAPPING YOUR PERSONAL WINDOW

Your window of tolerance isn't fixed—it expands and contracts based on various factors:

- Certain people who feel safe versus those who trigger you
- Physical environments that calm versus overstimulate you
- Time of day when you feel most regulated
- Life circumstances that support versus drain your capacity

John discovered his window was incredibly narrow after years of childhood emotional neglect. He would go from zero to explosive anger in seconds during conflicts with his partner, or completely shut down and become unreachable for days.

Through tracking his patterns, he realized his window expanded when he felt physically safe and contracted dramatically when he sensed any hint of criticism or abandonment.

These were echoes of his early experiences.

Understanding your window of tolerance is the foundation for everything that follows in your rewiring journey. As we move into befriending your inner child in the next phase, you'll use this awareness to create the safety your nervous system needs to heal and form secure connections.

TUNING INTO YOUR BODY'S WISDOM DAILY

Building nervous system awareness is like developing a new language—the language your body has been speaking all along, but which you're finally learning to understand. This awareness becomes the foundation for breaking free from unconscious reactive patterns that sabotage your relationships.

Your body holds incredible wisdom about what feels safe, what triggers old wounds, and what your system needs to heal. But most of us have been disconnected from this inner guidance system for so long that we've forgotten how to listen.

MORNING NERVOUS SYSTEM CHECK-INS

Start each day by placing a hand on your chest and belly, noticing your breath, heart rate, and overall sense of activation or calm. This isn't about judging what you find or immediately trying to fix anything—it's about gathering information.

Ask yourself simple questions:

- How fast or slow is my breathing?
- Does my body feel tense or relaxed?
- Am I holding stress anywhere specific?
- What does my energy level feel like right now?

HOURLY BODY SCANS THROUGHOUT THE DAY

Set gentle reminders to pause and notice what's happening in your shoulders, jaw, stomach, and breathing without trying to change anything. These micro check-ins help you catch stress before it builds into overwhelm or shutdown.

Pay attention to how different people, situations, and environments affect your nervous system. Notice patterns without judgment.

EVENING REGULATION PRACTICES

Wind down with gentle movement, warm baths, or progressive muscle relaxation to help your system transition into rest mode. This signals to your nervous system that the day is complete and it's safe to restore.

Patricia was amazed when she started her daily check-ins and realized she had been holding her breath for most of her adult life. Growing up with an alcoholic parent had taught her to be constantly vigilant, always scanning for danger.

Her morning practice of conscious breathing became a way of telling her nervous system, "You're safe now. You can relax."

This simple shift began to transform how she showed up in her romantic relationships—less guarded, more present, and able to receive love without immediately bracing for disappointment. The daily practice created a new baseline of safety that made deeper intimacy possible.

CATCHING YOUR TRIGGERS IN REAL TIME

The space between stimulus and response is where your freedom lives. Most people with anxious or avoidant attachment patterns have lost access to this space—they react from their nervous system's alarm bells before their conscious mind even knows what's happening.

Learning to catch activation early is like installing an early warning system for your emotional responses.

When you're dancing the anxiety-avoidance tango we explored in Chapter 3, your triggers often feel like they come out of nowhere. One moment you're fine, the next you're flooded with panic about your partner's text tone or completely shutting down because they want to have a serious conversation.

But triggers don't actually come out of nowhere. They have a buildup period.

PHYSICAL EARLY WARNING SIGNS

Your body starts responding before your mind catches up. Learn to recognize tension in specific body parts, changes in breathing, temperature shifts, or digestive responses that happen before emotional overwhelm hits.

Common physical signals include:

- Shoulders rising toward your ears
- Jaw clenching or teeth grinding
- Stomach dropping or churning
- Hands getting cold or sweaty
- Heart rate increasing subtly

MENTAL AND EMOTIONAL PRECURSORS

Notice racing thoughts, sudden mood drops, irritability, or the urge to withdraw or attack before you're fully activated. These mental shifts often happen alongside physical changes.

You might experience:

- Thoughts speeding up or becoming repetitive
- Sudden urges to escape or control the situation
- Feeling like your partner is "too much" or "not enough"

- Old stories about abandonment or criticism flooding back

BEHAVIORAL PATTERN RECOGNITION

Notice your go-to responses when activation begins. Do you get busy, pick fights, go silent, or seek reassurance? Everyone has unique patterns.

Adam learned to recognize that his jaw would clench and his shoulders would rise toward his ears about thirty seconds before he would either explode in anger or completely withdraw from his partner.

This tiny window of awareness became his gateway to choice.

Instead of being hijacked by his nervous system's ancient programming from growing up with critical, demanding parents, he could pause and ask himself: "What does this situation actually require? What would love look like right now?"

This skill sets the foundation for the inner child work we'll explore next.

BREATHE YOUR WAY TO BODY SAFETY

Your nervous system learns safety through experience, not through thinking. After years or decades of operating from survival mode, you need to actively teach your body what safety feels like through practices that engage your parasympathetic nervous system—your rest, digest, and connect system.

These practices become your daily medicine for rewiring attachment patterns at the deepest level.

COHERENT BREATHING TECHNIQUES

Practice breathing in for 4-6 counts and out for 6-8 counts to activate your vagus nerve and signal safety to your system. This simple rhythm tells your nervous system that you're not in danger and can move out of hypervigilance or shutdown.

Start with just five minutes daily:

- Inhale slowly through your nose for 4 counts
- Exhale gently through your mouth for 6 counts
- Focus on making your exhale longer than your inhale
- Let your belly expand on the inhale, contract on the exhale

GENTLE MOVEMENT PRACTICES

Yoga, walking, dancing, or stretching help discharge stored activation and reconnect you with your body's wisdom. Movement that feels good to your system helps complete stress cycles that may have been stuck for years.

Choose activities that feel nurturing rather than punishing. This isn't about fitness goals—it's about befriending your body.

PROGRESSIVE MUSCLE RELAXATION

Systematically tense and release different muscle groups to help your nervous system experience the contrast between activation and relaxation. Start with your feet and work up to your head, holding tension for five seconds, then releasing completely.

This practice teaches your body the difference between holding stress and letting it go.

Lisa had always been disconnected from her body, living primarily in her head as a survival strategy from childhood emotional abuse.

When she began incorporating daily breathwork and gentle yoga into her routine, she described it as "coming home to myself."

For the first time in years, she could feel her own needs, boundaries, and desires clearly.

This embodied self-awareness became the foundation for attracting and maintaining the healthy, secure love she had always craved but never felt worthy of receiving.

These practices prepare your nervous system for the deeper inner child work we'll explore next, where you'll learn to provide the safety and nurturing your younger self never received.

5
REWIRING DAY 8-14: BEFRIENDING YOUR INNER CHILD

HEALING THE HIDDEN WOUNDS BEHIND LOVE

Picture a seven-year-old hiding in a closet, listening to their parents fight, promising themselves they'll never need anyone so they won't get hurt. That child's survival strategy becomes the adult's relationship blueprint—until we learn to access and heal these wounded parts that unconsciously drive our patterns.

Your wounded inner child holds the key to understanding why you keep attracting unavailable partners, why you push people away when they get close, or why you lose yourself in relationships. These parts of you aren't broken—they're brilliant survival mechanisms that once protected you but now sabotage your adult connections. Learning to access them with curiosity rather than judgment is the first step toward transformation.

Now that you've spent the first week building awareness of your nervous system responses, you're ready to go deeper. The patterns you noticed—the fight-or-flight reactions, the freeze responses, the people-pleasing—all have roots in younger parts of yourself that learned these strategies for good reasons.

Identifying Your Protective Patterns

Notice when you feel triggered in relationships—the sudden urge to flee, the compulsion to control, or the desperate need for reassurance. These reactions often stem from specific childhood wounds that created protective strategies.

Recognizing the Age of Your Triggers

When you're activated, ask yourself "How old do I feel right now?" Often, our emotional reactions correspond to specific developmental stages where we experienced disruption or trauma.

Creating Safety for Emergence

Wounded parts only reveal themselves when they feel safe. This requires developing a compassionate, non-judgmental inner observer who can witness your patterns without shame or criticism.

Margaret discovered that her pattern of dating emotionally unavailable men traced back to age four, when her father left without explanation. The wounded part of her believed that if she could just be perfect enough, she could make someone stay.

Through accessing this younger part with compassion, she began to understand that her adult relationships were attempts to heal this original abandonment wound. As she learned to give her four-year-old self the reassurance and love she needed, her attraction to unavailable partners began to shift.

This inner child work prepares you for the next phase of rewiring, where you'll begin rewriting the love scripts these younger parts created.

HEALING CONVERSATIONS WITH YOUR YOUNGER SELF

Every morning, Lucas began setting aside ten minutes to check in with his inner child—the part of him that felt unseen and unheard growing up with critical parents. This simple practice of daily dialogue transformed not only his relationship with himself but his capacity for intimate connection with others.

Inner child dialogue isn't about regression or dwelling in the past—it's about developing a nurturing relationship with the younger parts of yourself that still influence your adult behavior. When you consistently show up for your inner child with presence and care, you build the internal security that allows for healthy, secure love in your external relationships.

Building on the nervous system awareness you developed in week one, this second week focuses on creating consistent, caring communication with your wounded parts. Your nervous system responses revealed where these younger parts get activated. Now you'll learn to dialogue with them directly.

Morning Check-ins

Start each day by asking your inner child how they're feeling and what they need. Listen without trying to fix or change anything—simply offer presence and validation. This creates the foundation of internal security.

Evening Comfort Rituals

End your day by offering your younger self comfort and reassurance, especially after difficult interactions or triggering events. This might involve gentle self-talk, physical comfort, or visualization exercises that soothe activated parts.

Consistent Emotional Attunement

Throughout the day, notice when you feel small, scared, or reactive, and respond with the same care you'd give a beloved child—patience, understanding, and gentle guidance rather than criticism or dismissal.

Samantha struggled with people-pleasing that left her exhausted and resentful in relationships. Through daily inner child work, she discovered that her six-year-old self had learned that being "good" was the only way to receive love and avoid conflict.

Each morning, she would tell this younger part: "You don't have to earn love anymore. You're worthy just as you are."

Over time, this consistent reparenting helped her set boundaries and express her needs authentically, attracting partners who valued her true self rather than her performance.

This foundation of self-compassion and internal security prepares you for the next phase: consciously rewriting the love scripts these younger parts created to survive.

HEALING THE CHILD WITHIN YOU

When Marcus was eight years old, he came home excited about winning a school art contest, only to have his achievement dismissed by parents too stressed and overwhelmed to celebrate with him. Forty years later, he still struggled to share good news with partners, unconsciously protecting himself from potential disappointment. The healing came when he learned to give his eight-year-old self the celebration and recognition he had needed.

Reparenting involves identifying the specific emotional nutrients your younger self was deprived of and consistently providing them now. This isn't about blaming your caregivers or changing the past—it's about taking responsibility for meeting your own emotional needs so you can show up as a whole, secure person in your relationships.

After two weeks of nervous system awareness and inner child dialogue, you're ready for active reparenting. The conversations you've been having with your younger parts have revealed what they needed then and still need now. This week focuses on giving your inner child those missing experiences.

Identifying Core Unmet Needs

Common childhood needs include safety, validation, unconditional love, appropriate boundaries, emotional attunement, and encouragement. Reflect on which of these were missing or inconsistent in your early experience.

Providing Consistent Emotional Nourishment

If you needed more affection, practice loving self-touch and verbal affirmations. If you needed validation, acknowledge your feelings and experiences without judgment. If you needed safety, create predictable routines and environments that feel secure.

Healing Through Corrective Experiences

Actively seek out and create experiences that provide what was missing. This might mean joining communities where you feel seen, engaging in activities that bring joy, or learning to receive care from others.

Rebecca grew up in a household where emotions were seen as weakness, leaving her unable to express vulnerability in adult relationships. She began reparenting by holding space for all of her feelings —anger, sadness, fear, and joy—with the same acceptance she would offer a child.

She practiced saying "It makes sense that you feel this way" to her emotional experiences.

As she developed this internal emotional safety, she found herself able to share her authentic feelings with her partner, deepening their intimacy and connection. This inner security becomes the foundation for rewriting your love scripts entirely.

FROM INNER CRITIC TO GENTLE GUIDE

The voice in David's head sounded exactly like his perfectionist mother: "You're not good enough. You'll never find someone who truly loves you. You're too sensitive, too needy, too much." This internalized criticism had sabotaged every relationship, creating a self-fulfilling prophecy of rejection and abandonment. The transformation began when he learned to recognize this voice as his wounded inner child's misguided attempt at protection, not truth.

Inner criticism often develops as a child's attempt to prevent future hurt by controlling behavior and anticipating rejection. While this voice believes it's protecting you, it actually perpetuates the very patterns that create relationship difficulties. Learning to transform criticism into compassionate guidance breaks the cycle of self-sabotage and opens space for secure, loving connection.

As you've been dialoguing with your inner child and providing reparenting, you've likely noticed a harsh internal voice trying to sabotage this healing work. This critic represents another wounded part that needs your attention and compassion.

Recognizing the Critic's Protective Function

Your inner critic isn't evil—it's usually a young part trying to keep you safe from rejection, abandonment, or failure. Understanding its positive intention helps you respond with compassion rather than resistance.

Developing the Compassionate Inner Parent

Cultivate a wise, loving internal voice that can offer guidance without shame or attack. This voice validates your experience while gently encouraging growth and healing.

Reframing Critical Thoughts

When you notice self-attack, pause and ask: "What is this young part afraid of?" Then offer reassurance and guidance from your adult self, addressing the underlying fear with love and understanding.

Rachel discovered that her harsh inner critic developed after her parents' divorce when she was ten, believing that if she could just be perfect, she could prevent future loss and abandonment. This voice drove her to overachieve in relationships, exhausting herself trying to be the "perfect" partner.

Through inner child work, she learned to recognize when this young part was activated and respond with gentleness: "Sweet one, you don't have to be perfect to be loved. You're enough just as you are."

As her self-compassion grew, she attracted a partner who loved her authentic self, flaws and all. This internal transformation sets the stage for rewriting your entire approach to love.

6

REWIRING DAY 15-21: REWRITING YOUR LOVE SCRIPT

UNCOVERING THE STORIES YOU TELL YOURSELF

Grace sat in her therapist's office, frustrated after another relationship ended the same way. "I don't understand," she said. "I keep attracting the same type of unavailable men." Her therapist gently asked, "What did you learn about love growing up?" The question stopped her cold. For the first time, Grace began to see the invisible script that had been running her love life for decades.

Your unconscious relationship beliefs are the hidden operating system of your romantic life. These deeply embedded assumptions about love, relationships, and your worthiness were formed in childhood and continue to influence every romantic choice you make. Most people are completely unaware of these beliefs, yet they dictate everything from whom you're attracted to, how you behave in relationships, and even how relationships end.

After spending the past week befriending your inner child, you're now ready to examine the stories that child learned about love. These stories became your relationship blueprint.

The Three Core Areas to Explore:

- Excavating childhood love lessons: Examine the spoken and unspoken messages you received about love from your primary caregivers, including how they treated each other and how they treated you during emotional moments.
- Recognizing your relationship patterns: Track the common themes across your romantic relationships - the types of people you attract, how conflicts unfold, and how relationships typically end.
- Challenging limiting love beliefs: Question beliefs like "love hurts," "I'm not worthy of lasting love," or "people always leave" by examining the evidence for and against these assumptions.

Ethan discovered his unconscious belief was "I have to be perfect to be loved" after his mother consistently withdrew affection when he made mistakes as a child. This belief drove him to be a people-pleaser in relationships, constantly anxious about disappointing his partners. By recognizing this pattern, he could finally understand why his relationships felt exhausting and why partners eventually felt suffocated by his need for constant reassurance.

The awareness alone began to loosen the grip this belief had on his romantic choices.

This week focuses on bringing these invisible scripts into the light. Once you can see them clearly, you can begin rewriting them. The goal isn't to judge these beliefs harshly - they served a purpose in childhood.

Now it's time to create new ones.

REWIRING YOUR BRAIN WITH MENTAL PRACTICE

Every morning, Rachel would close her eyes and visualize herself in a loving, secure relationship. She saw herself communicating openly without fear, receiving love without suspicion, and giving love without losing herself. At first, these images felt foreign, almost impossible. But after weeks of practice, something shifted. The scenes began to feel more natural, more attainable. Her nervous system was learning a new way of being in love.

Your brain's neuroplasticity means you can literally rewire your relationship patterns by consistently practicing new thoughts and behaviors. Visualization and affirmation work by creating new neural pathways that compete with old, destructive patterns. When you repeatedly imagine yourself in healthy relationship scenarios, your brain begins to recognize these patterns as familiar and safe, making them more likely to manifest in real life.

Now that you've befriended your inner child and uncovered your limiting love stories, it's time to install new programming. Mental rehearsal is one of the most powerful tools for creating lasting change.

Three Core Mental Practice Techniques:

- Daily relationship visualization: Spend 10-15 minutes each day visualizing yourself in specific secure relationship scenarios - having difficult conversations with ease, receiving love gracefully, or maintaining your independence within partnership.
- Embodied affirmations: Create affirmations that address your specific attachment wounds, such as "I am worthy of consistent, reliable love" or "I can be loved for who I am, not what I do," and repeat them while feeling the emotions they evoke.

- Future self meditation: Regularly connect with your future self who has healed attachment patterns, asking for guidance and absorbing the energy of someone who loves and receives love securely.

Jonathan struggled with avoidant attachment patterns that made him withdraw whenever relationships became too intimate. He began visualizing himself staying present during emotional conversations instead of shutting down. He would imagine feeling his partner's emotions without being overwhelmed, responding with curiosity instead of defensiveness. After three weeks of daily practice, he noticed that when his girlfriend wanted to discuss their future, instead of his usual urge to flee, he felt curious about her perspective.

The new neural pathway was beginning to compete with the old pattern of emotional withdrawal.

This mental practice prepares your nervous system for the final phase of transformation - becoming magnetically secure in your daily interactions.

BUILDING YOUR SECURE ATTACHMENT TOOLKIT

Sarah had always been anxiously attached, constantly seeking reassurance from partners. But during her healing journey, she committed to daily practices that helped her embody security. She started each morning by placing her hand on her heart and reminding herself of her inherent worthiness. Throughout the day, she practiced self-soothing when anxiety arose instead of immediately reaching for her phone to text her partner. These small, consistent actions gradually shifted her from anxious to secure.

Secure attachment isn't just a mindset - it's a set of behaviors and emotional responses that can be learned and practiced. By consistently engaging in secure attachment behaviors, even when they feel unnatural at first, you begin to embody the energy of someone who is comfortable with intimacy and independence simultaneously.

After spending weeks befriending your inner child and rewriting your love scripts through mental practice, you're now ready to build practical tools for daily life. These aren't theory - they're concrete actions that create secure attachment in real time.

Your Essential Secure Attachment Toolkit:

- Self-soothing practices: Develop a toolkit of techniques to calm your nervous system when attachment anxiety or avoidance is triggered, including breathwork, grounding exercises, and self-compassion practices.
- Emotional regulation techniques: Learn to pause and process emotions before reacting, creating space between trigger and response that allows for more conscious relationship choices.
- Secure communication patterns: Practice expressing needs directly, listening without defending, and staying present during difficult conversations rather than shutting down or becoming reactive.

Michael realized his avoidant tendencies were actually a nervous system response to perceived emotional overwhelm. He began practicing staying present when his girlfriend expressed strong emotions instead of immediately planning his escape. He would breathe deeply, remind himself that her emotions weren't dangerous, and ask curious questions instead of offering solutions or withdrawing. Over time, these practices helped him develop the capacity to be emotionally available without losing himself, a hallmark of secure attachment.

The beauty of this toolkit is that each practice reinforces the others. When you learn to self-soothe, emotional regulation becomes easier. When you can regulate your emotions, secure communication flows naturally.

This foundation prepares you for the final phase of transformation - becoming magnetically secure in all your relationships.

LOVE WITHOUT FEAR OR FLIGHT

When Lauren first tried to simply receive a compliment from her partner without deflecting or immediately reciprocating, she felt physically uncomfortable. Her body had learned that receiving love was dangerous - it meant vulnerability, potential disappointment, possible abandonment. But she practiced anyway, breathing through the discomfort and allowing herself to simply say "thank you" and feel the warmth of being appreciated. Gradually, receiving love became less terrifying and more nourishing.

The ability to give and receive love freely is the cornerstone of secure attachment. Most people with attachment wounds have learned dysfunctional patterns around love exchange - giving too much to earn love, being unable to receive without suspicion, or withholding love to maintain control. Learning to love without these protective strategies requires rewiring both your nervous system and your behavioral patterns.

After building your secure attachment toolkit, you're ready to practice the most vulnerable aspect of healing - loving without the armor of fear or the escape route of avoidance.

Three Essential Love Skills:

- Receiving love practices: Learn to accept compliments, affection, and support without immediately deflecting, reciprocating, or questioning the giver's motives, allowing yourself to simply absorb the love offered.

- Giving love authentically: Practice expressing love from genuine desire rather than fear, obligation, or manipulation, ensuring your giving comes from overflow rather than depletion.
- Love without conditions: Challenge the unconscious belief that love must be earned or maintained through performance by practicing loving and being loved for simply existing, not for what you do or provide.

Marcus had learned to give love through acts of service and problem-solving, but struggled with emotional intimacy and verbal affection. His partner craved emotional connection and words of affirmation, but these felt foreign and vulnerable to him. He began practicing small expressions of emotional availability - sharing one feeling each day, offering verbal appreciation, and expressing affection without it being tied to physical intimacy. Initially, it felt awkward and forced, but over time, emotional expression became a natural part of how he showed love, deepening their connection significantly.

This practice of loving without protective strategies prepares you for the final transformation phase - becoming magnetically secure in all your relationships.

7
REWIRING DAY 22-30: BECOMING MAGNETICALLY SECURE

LIVING YOUR NEW CONNECTION STYLE

The final week of your transformation marks a profound shift from practicing secure attachment to simply being securely attached. Your new connection style becomes as natural as breathing, flowing through every interaction without conscious effort or second-guessing.

CREATING AUTOMATIC SECURE RESPONSES

Your nervous system now recognizes healthy connection as the default setting. When Lauren received a delayed text response from her boyfriend, she noticed her first thought was "He must be busy" rather than "What did I do wrong?" This automatic secure interpretation happened without any deliberate reframing techniques from earlier weeks.

The key lies in consistent repetition until secure responses become muscle memory:

- Trust as first instinct - Assuming positive intent becomes your natural response
- Calm communication - Speaking from centered energy rather than reactive emotions
- Healthy boundaries - Saying no feels comfortable and necessary, not guilty
- Emotional regulation - Big feelings don't derail your sense of self-worth

ESTABLISHING NEW RELATIONSHIP RITUALS

Daily practices now reinforce your secure foundation automatically. Mason created a ritual of expressing one appreciation to his partner each evening, which strengthened their bond while reinforcing his own secure mindset.

Your rituals might include:

- Morning intention setting for loving connection
- Evening gratitude sharing with your partner
- Weekly relationship check-ins without drama
- Monthly celebration of growth milestones

TRANSFORMING YOUR INNER DIALOGUE

Notice how your internal voice has shifted. Where self-doubt once lived, curiosity now thrives. Instead of "Why don't they love me enough?" your mind asks "What would feel most loving right now?"

This inner transformation creates ripple effects throughout your life. Lauren found herself attracting new friendships that matched her secure energy, while old relationships either deepened or naturally faded away.

Your secure attachment style now acts as a magnet, drawing in people who appreciate authentic connection while repelling those who thrive on drama or emotional unavailability.

The work you've done over these thirty days has created lasting neurological changes.

You're ready for the next phase: becoming a secure partner magnet.

MAGNETIC ENERGY THAT DRAWS HEALTHY LOVE

Your transformation into secure attachment creates a profound energetic shift that fundamentally changes who you attract and who attracts you. This isn't mystical thinking—it's the natural result of how your nervous system now communicates safety and emotional availability to others.

DEVELOPING AUTHENTIC CONFIDENCE

Secure attachment breeds genuine confidence that differs entirely from the performance-based confidence you might have relied on before. Amelia noticed that she stopped trying to impress potential partners with achievements or perfect appearance, instead feeling comfortable sharing her authentic thoughts and vulnerabilities from early conversations.

This authentic confidence manifests as:

- Comfortable silence - No need to fill every pause with nervous chatter
- Honest boundaries - Saying what you mean without apology or over-explanation
- Relaxed body language - Your nervous system signals safety to others

- Genuine curiosity - Asking questions because you're truly interested, not performing

RECOGNIZING SECURE ATTACHMENT SIGNALS

Your rewired nervous system now recognizes healthy attachment cues that you previously missed or dismissed. Gavin realized he was finally noticing when someone responded thoughtfully to his texts, maintained consistent communication, and showed genuine interest in his well-being rather than just excitement about chemistry.

Secure partners demonstrate:

- Consistent follow-through on plans and promises
- Comfortable discussing feelings without drama
- Respect for your boundaries and time
- Integration of you into their existing life rather than compartmentalization

BREAKING UNAVAILABLE ATTRACTION PATTERNS

Perhaps most remarkably, the people who once triggered your anxious or avoidant patterns now feel completely uninteresting. The hot-and-cold texter who would have consumed your thoughts for weeks now gets deleted without a second thought.

Your nervous system has learned to recognize red flags as turn-offs rather than challenges to overcome. Amelia laughed when she realized that the mysterious, emotionally unavailable types she once found irresistible now seemed exhausting and immature.

This shift happens because your attachment system now craves what actually feels good: consistency, emotional safety, and mutual respect.

The magnetic quality you've developed attracts partners who share these same values.

WHEN LIFE TESTS YOUR PROGRESS

Life will inevitably test your newfound secure attachment, and these moments don't represent failure—they're opportunities to strengthen your progress. Your nervous system occasionally remembers old patterns, especially during stress, but now you have tools to navigate these challenges gracefully.

IMPLEMENTING RAPID RECOVERY STRATEGIES

When triggers surface, your response time becomes everything. Marcus learned to catch himself mid-spiral when his girlfriend didn't respond to texts immediately, implementing what he called his "pause protocol" before old anxious patterns could take hold.

Your rapid recovery toolkit includes:

- The 4-7-8 breath - Four counts in, seven held, eight out to reset your nervous system
- Reality checking - Asking "What evidence supports this fear right now?"
- Grounding statements - "I am safe. This feeling will pass. I choose security."
- Physical movement - Walking, stretching, or gentle exercise to discharge activation

USING TRIGGERS AS INFORMATION

Instead of viewing emotional reactions as proof of your brokenness, you now recognize them as valuable data about your healing journey. When Sophia felt overwhelming jealousy about her partner's female coworker, she didn't shame herself for the feeling but explored what her inner child needed to feel safe.

Triggers reveal:

- Areas still healing from past wounds
- Current relationship needs requiring attention
- Nervous system patterns needing additional rewiring
- Opportunities for deeper intimacy through vulnerability

MAINTAINING PERSPECTIVE AND SELF-COMPASSION

The most significant change isn't the absence of difficult emotions—it's how you relate to them when they arise. You no longer catastrophize temporary setbacks or use them as evidence that you're fundamentally flawed.

Marcus found himself thinking, "This anxious feeling means I'm human, not broken" instead of his old thought pattern of "I'll never be good enough for love." This shift in internal dialogue prevented single moments of insecurity from becoming relationship disasters.

Your secure attachment foundation remains solid even when surface emotions feel turbulent.

These challenging moments actually deepen your security when handled with awareness and compassion rather than panic and shame.

BUILDING BONDS THAT LAST DAILY

Sustaining your secure attachment transformation requires intentional daily practices that keep your new neural pathways strong and prevent old patterns from creeping back in during stressful periods. These aren't burdensome rituals but simple, nurturing habits that become as natural as brushing your teeth.

MORNING MINDFULNESS ROUTINES

Starting your day from a secure foundation shapes every interaction that follows. Rachel discovered that spending just five minutes each morning setting an intention for loving connection completely changed how she showed up in her relationships throughout the day.

Your morning practice might include:

- Gratitude for current relationships - Appreciating what's working builds positive neural pathways
- Intention setting - Choosing how you want to show up securely today
- Body awareness - Checking in with your nervous system's baseline
- Affirmation of worth - Reminding yourself you deserve healthy love

EVENING REFLECTION PRACTICES

Processing your relationship experiences each evening prevents unresolved emotions from accumulating and triggering old patterns. David found that his brief evening review helped him celebrate small wins while identifying areas for gentle improvement.

Effective evening practices include:

- Three connection moments - Recalling times you felt genuinely connected to others
- One secure response - Acknowledging where you showed up differently than before
- Growth opportunity - Noting one area for tomorrow's improvement without self-criticism

- Emotional release - Letting go of any relationship stress from the day

WEEKLY RELATIONSHIP CHECK-INS

Consistent weekly reviews prevent small issues from becoming major problems while reinforcing your commitment to secure patterns. These sessions help you course-correct quickly when old habits surface.

Your weekly check-in should address:

- Current relationship satisfaction levels
- Any triggers or patterns that emerged
- Communication successes and areas needing attention
- Goals for deeper connection in the coming week

These practices create a sustainable foundation for lifelong secure attachment.

They're your insurance policy against regression and your pathway to continuously deeper, more fulfilling relationships as you move forward in your transformed life.

8

THE SECURE PARTNER MAGNET PROTOCOL

WHEN SECURITY BECOMES YOUR RELATIONSHIP MAGNET

After spending the past thirty days rewiring your attachment patterns and becoming magnetically secure, you're now operating from a completely different energetic frequency. This shift creates what researchers call the "secure partner magnet effect."

When you operate from secure attachment, you naturally attract other emotionally healthy individuals while repelling those who remain stuck in anxious or avoidant cycles. This isn't about becoming perfect or never experiencing relationship challenges.

It's about fundamental changes in how you show up.

You now communicate your needs directly without manipulation tactics or passive-aggressive behavior. Instead of hoping your partner will read your mind or dropping hints that create confusion, you express yourself clearly and kindly. This directness creates safety for both partners to be authentic.

Your boundaries have transformed from rigid walls or complete absence into healthy, flexible limits. These boundaries protect your energy while remaining open to genuine connection. You can say no without guilt and yes without resentment.

Conflict no longer feels like a threat to the relationship's survival. You approach disagreements as opportunities for deeper understanding and growth together. This shift changes everything about how potential partners experience you.

The Magnet Protocol includes:

- Direct communication without emotional manipulation
- Healthy boundaries that invite connection
- Conflict resolution skills that strengthen rather than damage bonds
- Emotional regulation that creates stability
- Self-awareness that prevents projection

Jennifer experienced this transformation firsthand. After six months of attachment healing work, she noticed completely different types of partners entering her life. Where she once attracted emotionally unavailable men who triggered her anxious patterns, she now connected with Jackson, a secure partner who appreciated her directness and emotional availability.

When Jennifer expressed concerns about their relationship timeline, instead of withdrawing or becoming defensive like her previous partners, Jackson listened actively and worked collaboratively to address her needs. His response demonstrated the secure attachment she had been unconsciously seeking all along.

This magnetic shift happens because secure individuals recognize and value emotional health in others. They're drawn to partners who can communicate clearly, handle emotions maturely, and maintain their identity within relationship dynamics.

Your new secure foundation naturally filters out incompatible matches while attracting those ready for genuine partnership.

TRUE SAFETY VERSUS COMFORTABLE ILLUSIONS

Your nervous system has been programmed to recognize certain patterns as "love," even when those patterns represent trauma bonds or anxious attachment dynamics rather than genuine connection. This creates a dangerous confusion between intensity and intimacy, between familiar dysfunction and actual safety.

Learning to distinguish between real security and comfortable illusions requires rewiring your internal recognition system completely.

For years, you may have mistaken drama for passion, inconsistency for excitement, and emotional unavailability for mystery. Your body learned to associate the rush of anxiety with romance, creating addictive cycles that felt like love but were actually stress responses.

Secure partners initially feel unsettling because they lack the intensity you've been conditioned to crave. They don't create emotional roller coasters with devastating lows followed by intoxicating highs. Instead, they offer something your nervous system hasn't learned to value: consistent, reliable care.

Signs of genuine safety versus familiar dysfunction:

- Secure partners demonstrate consistency between words and actions over extended periods
- They respect your boundaries without seeing them as personal rejection or attempts at control

- Communication remains calm and solution-focused during disagreements
- They don't use love-bombing tactics followed by withdrawal patterns
- Your nervous system feels regulated rather than constantly activated in their presence

Caleb had always been drawn to partners who created emotional chaos—intense connections followed by devastating periods of distance that kept him anxious and hooked. When he met Penelope, a secure partner, his first instinct was dismissing her as "boring" or "not exciting enough."

She didn't play games, responded to texts consistently, and never made him wonder where he stood. She expressed her feelings directly without dramatic displays or manipulation tactics. His nervous system, accustomed to constant activation, interpreted this stability as lack of chemistry.

It took several weeks for Caleb to recognize that the calm, steady feeling he experienced with Penelope wasn't boredom—it was actual safety. His nervous system had never learned to identify emotional regulation as desirable or romantic.

This recognition represents a crucial turning point in your healing journey.

True safety feels different from what you've known. It's quieter, more consistent, and infinitely more nourishing than the addictive intensity of insecure attachment patterns you've mistaken for love.

BUILDING LOVE BEYOND OLD PATTERNS

Operating from secure attachment means showing up authentically from your very first interaction, establishing appropriate boundaries, and refusing to participate in manipulation games that once felt completely normal. This foundation creates opportunities to heal childhood wounds by experiencing relationships that actually prove your worth.

You're no longer trapped in the extremes that defined your old patterns.

Instead of oversharing intimate details too quickly or keeping partners at arm's length for months, you share vulnerabilities at a pace that matches the developing trust. This measured approach protects your heart while allowing genuine intimacy to grow naturally.

You maintain your own interests, friendships, and personal identity while building meaningful connection. Gone are the days of losing yourself completely in someone else's world or remaining so independent that no one can truly reach you.

When concerns arise, you address them directly rather than dropping hints and hoping they'll be understood or avoiding conflict entirely until resentment builds. This direct communication prevents the small issues from becoming relationship-ending problems.

Secure relationship building includes:

- Progressive vulnerability that matches earned trust levels
- Maintaining personal boundaries without creating walls
- Direct communication about needs and concerns
- Preserving individual identity within growing connection
- Choosing consistency over intensity in early stages

Sarah used to swing between two extremes in her dating approach. Sometimes she revealed everything about her traumatic childhood on first dates, overwhelming potential partners with her anxious need for immediate deep connection. Other times, she kept partners completely at arm's length for months, her avoidant patterns preventing any real intimacy from developing.

From her newly secure foundation, Sarah learned a different way. When Marcus asked about her family during their third date, she shared that her parents had divorced when she was young and it had been challenging, without diving into the complete story of her father's abandonment and her mother's subsequent depression.

This measured approach allowed intimacy to build naturally while protecting her heart appropriately. She could gauge Marcus's response to smaller vulnerabilities before sharing deeper wounds. Each interaction became an opportunity to practice healthy relationship skills rather than repeat old trauma patterns.

Building love beyond old patterns means creating new neural pathways through different experiences that prove you deserve consistent, healthy care.

FROM WARNING SIGNS TO WELCOME SIGNS

Your secure nervous system becomes highly attuned to both warning signs and positive indicators that you previously missed or completely misinterpreted. Red flags that once felt exciting or comfortably familiar now register as genuinely uncomfortable, while green flags that once seemed boring now feel deeply attractive and trustworthy.

This shift represents a fundamental rewiring of your attraction patterns.

Inconsistent communication patterns now feel unsettling rather than intriguing or normal. When someone takes days to respond without explanation, your secure foundation recognizes this as incompatibility rather than mystery to solve.

Love-bombing and excessive early intensity trigger your awareness systems rather than your attachment responses. Instead of feeling flattered by overwhelming attention, you notice the manipulation tactics and boundary violations these behaviors represent.

Genuine interest in your thoughts, feelings, and experiences feels attractive rather than suffocating. When someone asks meaningful questions and remembers your answers, you recognize this as healthy engagement instead of intrusive behavior.

Your new recognition system identifies:

- Consistency in words and actions as attractive stability
- Respectful responses to boundaries as green flags
- Calm, regulated energy as appealing rather than boring
- Direct communication as trustworthy rather than harsh
- Emotional availability as desirable rather than overwhelming

Marcus met someone who seemed perfect on paper but noticed she would disappear for days without explanation, then return with elaborate stories and grand gestures. His old anxious pattern would have been chasing harder during disappearances and feeling grateful for the dramatic returns.

Instead, his secure nervous system registered the inconsistency as clear incompatibility. The push-pull dynamic that once felt like passionate connection now felt exhausting and unstable.

When he later met Rachel, who texted back within reasonable time-frames and followed through on plans consistently, he recognized these "boring" qualities as green flags of someone capable of building stable, lasting relationships.

Rachel's steady presence didn't trigger his anxiety or create addictive intensity cycles. She expressed interest without overwhelming him, maintained her own life while building connection, and addressed concerns directly without drama or manipulation.

These qualities, which his anxious attachment might have dismissed as lack of chemistry, now registered as exactly what his healed nervous system craved: genuine safety, consistency, and the foundation for authentic intimacy to develop naturally over time.

9
WHEN OLD PATTERNS TRY TO HIJACK YOUR NEW LIFE

THE MESSY REALITY OF GETTING BETTER

Picture this: You've been doing the work, feeling more secure in your relationship, communicating better than ever before. Then one day, your partner comes home late without calling, and suddenly you're spiraling into the same anxious thoughts you thought you'd conquered. Your inner critic whispers, "See? You haven't changed at all."

This is the moment when many people abandon their healing journey.

Healing from insecure attachment patterns isn't like climbing a straight ladder to the top. It's more like walking up a mountain with switchbacks, plateaus, and occasional slides backward. Understanding this reality is crucial because it prevents you from catastrophizing temporary setbacks and helps you maintain compassion for yourself during the inevitable rough patches.

The Secure Partner Magnet Protocol you learned in the previous chapter works beautifully when life is steady. But real life rarely cooperates with our best intentions. Work stress hits. Family drama erupts. Money problems surface. These moments test everything you've built.

Key differences to recognize:

- Temporary regression - Old patterns surface but you notice them happening
- Complete relapse - Acting on every anxious or avoidant impulse without awareness
- Information gathering - Viewing setbacks as data about your triggers and growth edges
- Failure mindset - Believing one bad day erases months of progress

Rachel had been working on her anxious attachment for eight months when she experienced what felt like a complete breakdown. Her partner George had been unusually quiet for a few days due to work stress, and she found herself checking his phone, analyzing every text message, and creating elaborate stories about him losing interest.

"I felt like I was back at square one," she later reflected. "But my therapist helped me see that even though the anxious thoughts returned, I was now aware of them happening in real-time. Before, I would have acted on every anxious impulse without question. This time, I caught myself, talked to him about what I was experiencing, and we worked through it together."

The pattern showed up, but she had new tools to handle it.

This is progress disguised as failure. As you prepare to create your secure attachment legacy in our final chapter, remember that setbacks are not erasures of your growth.

MASTERING YOUR EMOTIONAL TRIPWIRES TOGETHER

Robert was having dinner with his girlfriend when she mentioned running into his ex at the coffee shop. Instantly, his chest tightened, his breathing became shallow, and he felt the familiar urge to shut down completely. In the past, he would have gone silent for days, leaving his girlfriend confused and hurt. But this time, he paused and said, "I'm feeling triggered right now. Can you give me five minutes to regulate myself, and then I'd like to talk about what just happened for me?"

This is what mastery looks like in real time.

When you've identified your core triggers and understand your attachment patterns from our earlier work together, the next step is developing sophisticated tools for managing those moments when your nervous system goes into overdrive. These aren't just basic coping mechanisms, but advanced techniques that help you stay present and connected even when every fiber of your being wants to run or fight.

The STOP Technique:

- Stop - Pause whatever you're doing or saying
- Take a breath - Activate your parasympathetic nervous system
- Observe - Notice what's happening in your body and mind
- Proceed - Move forward with intention rather than reaction

Co-regulation strategies work by using your partner's calm energy to help stabilize your own nervous system. This builds on the secure base concepts we explored when meeting your nervous system in the early days of rewiring.

Creating trigger action plans means having specific steps ready before you need them.

Catherine and her partner developed what they called their "yellow light system." When either of them felt triggered, they could call a "yellow light" - not a full stop like a red light, but a signal to slow down and proceed with extra care. During yellow light moments, they would lower their voices, make eye contact, and take turns sharing what was happening internally without trying to solve anything immediately.

"It gave us a way to acknowledge that someone was struggling without making it mean the relationship was in danger," Catherine explained. "We could stay connected while still honoring that one of us needed extra support."

This approach transforms triggers from relationship threats into opportunities for deeper intimacy. As we move into exploring your secure attachment legacy, these skills become the foundation for creating lasting change.

BREAKING FREE FROM COMMUNICATION AUTOPILOT

"I need you to text me more during the day," Michael told his partner, but even as the words left his mouth, he could hear the demanding tone that reminded him of his mother's anxious requests for constant reassurance. He paused and tried again: "I've noticed I feel more connected and secure when we check in with each other during the day. Would you be open to finding a texting rhythm that works for both of us?"

This moment illustrates a crucial breakthrough.

One of the biggest challenges in healing attachment wounds is learning to express your legitimate needs without falling back into the dysfunctional communication patterns you learned in childhood. Your needs are valid, but the way you learned to express them might push people away or create the very dynamic you're trying to avoid.

Remember the anxious-avoidant dance we explored earlier? Poor communication keeps that cycle spinning endlessly.

Key shifts in secure communication:

- Distinguishing between needs and strategies - What you need versus how you think it should be met
- Using "I" statements that invite connection rather than demand compliance
- Making requests rather than demands - Accepting "no" as valid information, not rejection
- Expressing the feeling underneath your complaint or criticism

This builds directly on the inner child work from your rewiring days. When you learned to befriend your inner child, you discovered that most complaints are actually unmet needs crying out for attention.

Sarah grew up in a household where needs were expressed through guilt, manipulation, and emotional outbursts. When she started dating recently, she found herself using the same tactics whenever she felt neglected. "I would say things like, 'You obviously don't care about me anymore' when what I really meant was 'I'm feeling disconnected and would love some quality time together,'" she recalls.

Learning to identify the feeling underneath her accusation and express it directly transformed her relationships. Instead of her partners becoming defensive, they could hear her actual need and respond with care.

The Secure Partner Magnet Protocol you mastered teaches you to attract secure partners, but maintaining that attraction requires breaking free from communication autopilot. When you express needs cleanly and directly, you create space for genuine intimacy to flourish.

This foundation becomes essential as we explore your secure attachment legacy in our final chapter.

GROWING TOGETHER WHILE STAYING WHOLE

David watched his girlfriend work through her own attachment healing and felt torn between two impulses: the desire to help her through every difficult moment, and the growing resentment that her healing journey seemed to consume all their conversations. He found himself walking on eggshells, afraid to bring up his own needs or concerns because she was "going through so much."

This scenario plays out in countless relationships where both partners are committed to growth.

When you're both healing, it's easy to fall into caretaking patterns where one person becomes the perpetual supporter and the other becomes the perpetual patient. This dynamic, while well-intentioned, can actually hinder both people's growth and create new forms of insecurity in the relationship.

Remember the inner child work we did during your rewiring days? Sometimes that wounded child wants to monopolize all the attention and care, leaving no room for your partner's needs.

Essential balance points:

- Maintaining your own boundaries while supporting your partner's healing journey

- Recognizing when support becomes enabling or codependency
- Creating space for both people's growth without making everything about attachment healing
- Sharing emotional labor equally rather than designating one person as the "broken" one

Lisa noticed that her partner had become increasingly quiet about his own struggles since she'd started therapy for her childhood trauma. When she asked him about it, he admitted he felt selfish bringing up his problems when hers seemed "so much bigger."

They realized they had unconsciously created a dynamic where her healing took precedence over his wellbeing.

Together, they established "growth check-ins" where they each had dedicated time to share their struggles and victories, ensuring both of their journeys received attention and support. "We learned that we could both be healing at the same time without competing for who needed more support," Lisa reflected.

This approach honors what you learned from the Secure Partner Magnet Protocol about maintaining your individual identity while building intimacy. Growing together doesn't mean losing yourself in your partner's process or expecting them to lose themselves in yours.

The goal is interdependence, not codependence.

As we move into exploring your secure attachment legacy, these skills for balanced growth become the foundation for creating relationships that can weather any storm while supporting both partners' continued evolution.

10
YOUR SECURE ATTACHMENT LEGACY

BREAKING CHAINS YOUR CHILDREN NEVER WORE

When Diana first began her secure attachment journey, she never imagined the ripple effect it would have on her family. Years later, watching her teenage daughter navigate her first relationship with healthy boundaries and clear communication, she realized that healing her own anxious patterns had literally changed the trajectory of her family's emotional DNA.

Your journey toward secure attachment doesn't end with you—it becomes a living legacy that transforms the emotional landscape for generations to come. By breaking free from anxious and avoidant patterns, you're not just healing yourself; you're interrupting cycles that may have persisted in your family for decades.

This is profound work.

The generational healing you accomplish through secure attachment rewiring creates ripple effects that extend far beyond your immediate relationships. When you learn to regulate your nervous system during conflict, your children witness what emotional stability looks like. When you practice expressing needs clearly instead of through anxious protests or avoidant withdrawal, you're modeling a completely different way of being in relationship.

Key ways your secure attachment creates generational change:

- Modeling secure communication patterns: Children and loved ones absorb how you handle conflict, express needs, and maintain boundaries, creating new templates for healthy relationships
- Breaking trauma transmission: Research shows that unhealed attachment wounds are often passed down through parenting styles, emotional regulation patterns, and relationship modeling
- Creating new family narratives: Your secure attachment practices establish fresh stories about what love, trust, and connection can look like in your family system

Jonathan grew up in a household where his father's avoidant tendencies meant emotional needs were rarely acknowledged, and his mother's anxious patterns created a constant undercurrent of tension. After implementing the rewiring techniques from previous chapters, he found himself naturally responding to his young son's emotional outbursts with patience and curiosity rather than dismissal or overwhelm.

His wife noticed the transformation immediately. "It's like watching a completely different kind of father emerge," she told him. "Our son feels so much safer expressing his feelings now."

Jonathan realized he had become the father he wished he'd had, breaking a cycle that had likely persisted for generations. The patterns that once hijacked his responses were now replaced with secure, grounded presence.

HEALING ROOTS WHILE GROWING FORWARD

Life has a way of testing our growth during major transitions—career changes, moves, relationship shifts, loss, and new beginnings all have the potential to activate old attachment patterns. The key to maintaining your secure attachment foundation lies in recognizing these vulnerable moments and having systems in place to support your continued growth.

Secure attachment isn't a destination you reach and then coast through life maintaining. It's a dynamic practice that requires ongoing attention, especially during periods of change and stress. By understanding how transitions can trigger childhood wounds and having tools ready to address these moments, you ensure that your progress continues to deepen rather than regress during challenging times.

Think of it as emotional immune system maintenance.

When your nervous system encounters significant change, it naturally scans for threats and may revert to familiar protective patterns—even if those patterns are the anxious or avoidant behaviors you've worked so hard to transform. This doesn't mean you've failed or lost your progress. It means you're human, and your attachment system is doing what it was designed to do: keep you safe.

Essential strategies for navigating transitions securely:

- Identifying transition triggers: Recognizing which types of changes are most likely to activate your old anxious or avoidant patterns
- Creating stability anchors: Establishing consistent practices, relationships, and routines that provide security during uncertain times
- Processing change through a secure lens: Developing the

ability to view transitions as opportunities for growth rather than threats to your safety

Susan thought she had her anxious attachment patterns well under control until her company announced a major restructuring. Suddenly, she found herself checking her phone obsessively for updates from her partner, seeking constant reassurance about their relationship even though the stress was work-related.

Rather than judging herself, she recognized this as her attachment system responding to threat and activated her support network. She scheduled extra therapy sessions, increased her mindfulness practice, and had honest conversations with her partner about needing additional emotional support during this transition.

By the time the work situation stabilized, she had actually deepened her secure attachment skills rather than regressing to old patterns. The transition became a catalyst for growth instead of a setback.

This is how secure attachment evolves—not through perfection, but through conscious response to life's inevitable challenges.

DESIGNING YOUR FOUNDATION FOR LASTING LOVE

Your environment either supports or undermines your secure attachment growth. Creating a life structure that reinforces your new patterns means being intentional about your relationships, routines, physical spaces, and daily practices. This isn't about perfection—it's about surrounding yourself with elements that make secure attachment the easier, more natural choice.

A secure attachment lifestyle requires more than just understanding the concepts—it needs to be woven into the fabric of your daily existence. This means evaluating everything from your living space to your social circle, from your work environment to your evening routines, asking whether each element supports or challenges your growth toward security.

Your foundation matters deeply.

Think of this as creating an ecosystem that naturally promotes the secure attachment behaviors you've been developing throughout your thirty-day rewiring journey. When your environment aligns with your growth goals, maintaining your progress becomes significantly easier because you're swimming with the current instead of against it.

Key areas for creating your secure attachment foundation:

- Curating supportive relationships: Gradually shifting your social circle to include more securely attached individuals while setting appropriate boundaries with those still operating from insecure patterns
- Designing your physical environment: Creating spaces that feel safe, nurturing, and conducive to emotional regulation and connection
- Establishing security-supporting routines: Building daily and weekly practices that reinforce your secure attachment skills, from morning mindfulness to regular relationship check-ins

Marcus realized that his Friday night routine of going to bars with college friends was actually undermining his secure attachment growth. These friends consistently engaged in relationship drama, complained about their partners without taking responsibility, and encouraged avoidant behaviors around commitment.

Instead of cutting them off entirely, he began suggesting different activities—hiking, dinner parties at his home, or attending cultural events—that created space for more meaningful connection. He also started hosting monthly dinners where friends could bring their partners, fostering an environment where healthy relationships were celebrated rather than mocked.

Over time, his social circle naturally evolved to include people who shared his values around secure, committed partnership. The shift wasn't dramatic or confrontational, but it was profound. His environment now reinforced the secure patterns he'd worked so hard to develop instead of constantly challenging them.

This is how lasting change happens—through intentional design of your daily life.

MODELING SECURE ATTACHMENT FOR OTHERS

The most powerful way to teach secure attachment isn't through lectures or advice—it's through the quiet consistency of your own embodied practice. When others witness your ability to navigate conflict with grace, communicate needs clearly, and maintain both intimacy and autonomy in relationships, they naturally become curious about what you're doing differently.

Your secure attachment journey positions you to be a beacon for others who are struggling with their own relationship patterns. This doesn't mean becoming a therapist or taking responsibility for others' healing, but rather living in such a way that your presence itself becomes an invitation to greater emotional health and relational security.

You become a living example.

This modeling happens through the countless small interactions that make up daily life—how you respond when someone is late, the way you express disappointment without attacking character, your ability to stay present during difficult conversations. These moments create a template for others to observe and potentially adopt in their own relationships.

Key ways you model secure attachment:

- Embodying secure responses in daily interactions: Consistently demonstrating healthy boundaries, emotional regulation, and clear communication in all your relationships
- Sharing your journey appropriately: Knowing when and how to discuss your attachment growth with others who express genuine interest
- Creating containers for deeper connection: Hosting gatherings, joining or forming groups, or engaging in activities that foster authentic relationship and emotional safety

Rebecca never intended to become the person her friends came to for relationship advice, but as her own partnership stabilized and flourished, she noticed others naturally gravitating toward her for support. Instead of offering quick fixes or taking on their emotional labor, she learned to share her experience while maintaining healthy boundaries.

"I used to think love meant constant anxiety and drama," she would tell friends. "Learning about attachment styles helped me understand that the chaos I thought was passion was actually just my nervous system being triggered."

She began hosting monthly women's circles where friends could share their relationship experiences in a supportive, non-judgmental environment, always emphasizing that each person's healing journey was their own responsibility.

Through these gatherings, Rebecca discovered that her most powerful teaching tool wasn't what she said, but how she showed up—calm, curious, and secure in herself while remaining genuinely connected to others.

CONCLUSION

Thirty days ago, you embarked on a transformative journey to break free from the anxious and avoidant relationship patterns that had been keeping you trapped in cycles of heartbreak and disappointment. You've worked courageously to heal deep childhood wounds that were sabotaging your adult relationships, and now you stand equipped with the knowledge and tools to attract and maintain healthy, secure love with genuine confidence.

This book was designed with a singular vision: to guide you through the scientific process of rewiring your attachment system from the ground up. You've learned that the relationship patterns you developed in childhood, while adaptive at the time, no longer serve your adult self. Through targeted neural rewiring techniques, daily practices, and deep inner work, you've begun the profound process of transforming your attachment style from insecure to secure.

The vision you're now living into is one where relationships become a source of joy, growth, and mutual support rather than anxiety, fear, and disappointment.

Throughout this 30-day journey, you've built a comprehensive foundation for secure attachment. Here are the key elements that have shaped your transformation:

- Meeting Your Nervous System: You learned to recognize activation signals and developed regulation techniques that create the calm foundation necessary for secure connection.
- Befriending Your Inner Child: You identified and began healing the early wounds that shaped your attachment patterns, using reparenting practices to give yourself what was missing.
- Rewriting Your Love Script: You examined and transformed the unconscious beliefs about relationships, replacing limiting narratives with empowering new stories about love.
- Becoming Magnetically Secure: You developed the authentic confidence and self-worth that naturally attracts other secure individuals while repelling unhealthy dynamics.

As you continue forward, these fundamental insights will serve as your guiding principles:

Security is a learnable skill that can be developed at any age through consistent practice. Your brain's neuroplasticity means the patterns you developed in childhood can be transformed through intentional effort. Healing happens in relationship with yourself first, creating the foundation for healthy connections with others.

Most importantly, your transformation creates ripple effects that extend far beyond romantic relationships.

Your 30-day journey is complete, but your growth continues. Here's your roadmap for maintaining and deepening your transformation:

- Continue Daily Practices: Commit to at least 15 minutes daily of nervous system regulation, inner child work, or secure attachment meditation.
- Seek Secure Relationships: Actively cultivate connections with people who celebrate your growth and support your continued healing.
- Share Your Story: When appropriate, let your transformation inspire others who might benefit from beginning their own healing journey.
- Trust Your New Instincts: The secure wisdom you've cultivated will guide you toward healthy relationship choices and away from old patterns.

As you close this book and step fully into your transformed life, take a moment to acknowledge the profound courage it took to begin this journey. Sophia recently shared that six months after completing her 30-day journey, she found herself in the healthiest relationship of her life. "I used to think I was broken," she said. "Now I realize I was just operating from old programming that no longer served me."

Howard wrote about how his relationship with his teenage daughter improved dramatically after practicing secure attachment. "When I healed my own patterns," he explained, "I stopped passing them on to her. I realized that healing myself was the greatest gift I could give her."

Your journey from insecure to secure attachment is one of the most profound gifts you can give yourself and the world. You are now equipped to love and be loved in ways you never thought possible. The neural pathways you've created will continue to strengthen with use. The healing you've initiated will continue to unfold in layers.

Trust the process. Trust yourself.

Your secure, loving future begins now.

www.ingramcontent.com/pod-product-compliance
Lightning Source LLC
LaVergne TN
LVHW090427210926
848480LV00002B/714

* 9 7 9 8 2 3 2 7 0 5 6 0 2 *